TRACTORS

by Darlene R. Stille

Content Adviser: MeeCee Baker, Ph.D., Adjunct Professor,
Department of Agricultural and Extension Education,
North Carolina State University
Reading Adviser: Dr. Linda D. Labbo,
Department of Reading Education, College of Education,
The University of Georgia

Compass Point Books

Minneapolis, Minnesota

Compass Point Books
3722 West 50th Street, #115
Minneapolis, MN 55410

Visit Compass Point Books on the Internet at *www.compasspointbooks.com* or e-mail your request to *custserv@compasspointbooks.com*

Editors: E. Russell Primm, Emily Dolbear, and Pam Rosenberg
Photo Researcher: Svetlana Zhurkina
Photo Selector: Linda S. Koutris
Designer: Melissa Voda

Library of Congress Cataloging-in-Publication Data
Stille, Darlene R.
    Tractors / by Darlene R. Stille.
        v. cm.— (Transportation / Darlene R. Stille)
    Summary: Briefly describes different kinds of tractors and other related machines and the work they do.
Includes bibliographical references and index.
    Contents: Who needs a tractor?—Why we need tractors—You need a small tractor—You need a farm tractor—You need a combine—You need a bulldozer—You need a power shovel—You need a backhoe— You need a front loader—You need a tractor with a crane—You need a snow plow tractor—You need a giant crawler.
    ISBN 0-7565-0287-X (hardcover)
        1. Tractors—Juvenile works. [1. Tractors.] I. Title.
    TL233.15 .S75 2002
    629.225'2—dc21   2002002953

Table of Contents

Who Needs a Tractor? _____ 5

Why Do We Need Tractors? _____ 6

You Need a Farm Tractor _____ 8

You Need a Lawn Tractor _____ 11

You Need a Combine _____ 13

You Need a Bulldozer _____ 14

You Need a Power Shovel _____ 17

You Need a Backhoe _____ 19

You Need a Front-End Loader _____ 21

You Need a Crawler with a Crane _____ 22

You Need a Snowplow Tractor _____ 25

You Need a Giant Crawler _____ 27

Glossary _____ 28

Did You Know? _____ 29

Want to Know More? _____ 30

Index _____ 32

Who Needs a Tractor?

Farmers need tractors. Miners also need tractors. People who build houses and roads need tractors, too.

Tractors can go almost anywhere. They can move about in mud and snow. Tractors hardly ever get stuck like cars or trucks do.

There are two kinds of tractors. One kind of tractor has big wheels. The other kind has no wheels. Instead, it has tracks that look like two big steel belts.

Tractors with tracks are called crawlers. An army tank is another kind of crawler.

Why Do We Need Tractors?

We need tractors to push or pull tools and machines.

Farmwork was harder before tractors were invented. Some farmers used horses to plow and plant seeds. The farmer walked behind the horse.

Digging and moving soil was hard work before tractors. Shovels were the only tools used for these jobs.

Tractors took the place of plows, shovels, and horses. Motors on the tractors do the hard work.

You Need a Farm Tractor

Do you want to help a farmer plant seeds? Then you need a farm tractor.

A farm tractor has four wheels. The wheels fit between the rows of plants.

Most big farm tractors have a cab. You sit inside the cab. It is air-conditioned and heated.

You hook tools to the tractor. The tools let the farmer plow or plant seeds. Tools help the farmer spray for bugs and weeds.

You Need a Lawn Tractor

Do you want to cut the grass? Do you want to plant trees in your yard? Then you need a lawn tractor. Lawn tractors can mow grass. They can also pull wagons filled with trees or soil.

You sit in front of the back wheels. You drive with a steering wheel. You press your foot on pedals to make the tractor stop and go.

You Need a Combine

Now the farmer needs to harvest the crop. You need a combine for this job.

A combine is a special kind of farm machine. It is used to cut down wheat or corn. A truck or tractor runs along beside the combine. The combine shoots the wheat or corn into the truck or tractor wagon.

You Need a Bulldozer

Do you want to make a road or build a house? Then you need a bulldozer to get the ground ready.

A bulldozer is a tractor with a big blade in the front. The blade goes up and down. Most bulldozers are crawler tractors.

Your bulldozer can knock down bushes and small trees. It can also push piles of dirt. Your bulldozer makes the ground smooth.

You Need a Power Shovel

Do you want to dig a big hole? You need a power shovel.

A power shovel is like a huge scoop with a long handle. It sits on a crawler.

A power shovel can dig long ditches. Miners use power shovels to dig up coal.

You sit in a cab on top of the tractor. You push and pull levers to work the shovel.

17

You Need a Backhoe

Do you want to dig a small hole? You need a backhoe.

A backhoe is a small tractor with wheels. It has a small bucket in back. It is like a small power shovel.

You Need a Front-End Loader

If you need to move a big pile of stones, you need a front-end loader.

A front-end loader is a small tractor with a bucket in front. You move the bucket up and down to pick up sand, stones, and dirt.

You Need a
Crawler with a Crane

How can you lift and move a car? You need a crane on a crawler! Cranes are like long arms with hooks, buckets, or straps.

A crane on a tractor can go anywhere and lift heavy things. You sit in a cab. You push and pull levers to make the crane go left or right, up or down.

You Need a Snowplow Tractor

A forest road is buried in deep snow.
A truck or a car would get stuck.

You need a special tractor for plowing this kind of snow. A snow-plow tractor may have wheels or tracks. It also has a big blade that pushes the snow away.

You Need a Giant Crawler

How do you move a rocket or a space shuttle? You need a giant tractor called a crawler-transporter.

Giant crawlers are the biggest tractors in the world. Tractors come in many sizes. There is one that is the right size for any job.

Glossary

levers—parts of machines that are like handles and are pushed or pulled to operate the machine

plow—to break up soil to make it ready for planting

space shuttle—a spacecraft used to take people and things back and forth from Earth to space

steel—a hard, strong metal made of iron and other materials

Did You Know?

The Tructor is an unusual truck with tractor features. It can seat three people and has a maximum speed of 25 miles (40 kilometers) per hour.

The first engine-powered farm tractors used steam and were introduced in 1868.

The tractor Henry Ford invented in 1907 was not called "tractor" at all. It was called an "automobile plow."

The Fordson was one of the first mass-produced tractors. It was made starting in 1916. Plowing speed was 2.8 miles (4.5 kilometers) per hour. It weighed more than a ton. It ran on kerosene and could plow 8 acres (3.25 hectares) on one tank of fuel!

Want to Know More?

At the Library

Brady, Peter. *Tractors*. Mankato, Minn.: Bridgestone Books, 1996.

Chandler, Gil. *Tractors*. Danbury, Conn.: Children's Press, 2000.

Mead, Sue. *Monster Trucks and Tractors*. Broomall, Penn.: Chelsea House, 1999.

Randolph, Joanne. *Bulldozers*. New York: Rosen Publishing Group, 2002.

On the Web

Antique Tractor Photos

http://www.antiquetractors.com/cgi-bin/gallery/photo_view.cgi

To see thousands of pictures of early tractors

Crawler-Transporter System

http://science.ksc.nasa.gov/facilities/crawler.html

For pictures and the story of how spacecraft are moved around on giant tractors at the Kennedy Space Center in Florida

John Deere Kids

http://www.deere.com/deerecom/_Kids/default.htm

For the story of Johnny Tractor and his pals, a farm-scene coloring book, and farm-safety tips for kids

Through the Mail
State Agricultural Heritage Museum

South Dakota State University

Box 2207C

Brookings, SD 57007-0999

To write for information about tractor exhibits and the early days of farming in the region

On the Road
Heritage Farmstead

1900 West 15th Street

Plano, TX 75025

972/424-7874

To visit a turn-of-the-century farm and museum

Index

backhoes, 19

bulldozers, 15

cabs, 9, 17, 23

coal mining, 17

combines, 13

cranes, 23

crawler-transporters, 27

crawlers, 5, 15, 17, 23, 27

farm tractors, 7, 9, 13

farmers, 5, 7, 13

front-end loaders, 21

harvest, 13

lawn tractors, 11

levers, 17, 23

miners, 5, 17

pedals, 11

power shovels, 17

shovels, 7, 17

snow-plow tractors, 25

space shuttle, 27

steering wheel, 11

tracks, 5, 25

wheels, 5, 9, 11, 25

About the Author

Darlene R. Stille is a science editor and writer. She has lived in Chicago, Illinois, all her life. When she was in high school, she fell in love with science. While attending the University of Illinois, she discovered that she also enjoyed writing. Today she feels fortunate to have a career that allows her to pursue both her interests. Darlene R. Stille has written more than thirty books for young people.